30408000004066

133.1
MAR

Martin, Michael.

Ghosts

The Unexplained

by **Michael Martin**

Consultant:
Andrew Nichols, PhD
Executive Director
American Institute of Parapsychology
Gainesville, Florida

Capstone
press

Mankato, Minnesota

Edge Books are published by Capstone Press
151 Good Counsel Drive, P.O. Box 669, Mankato, Minnesota 56002
www.capstonepress.com

Library of Congress Cataloging-in-Publication Data
Martin, Michael.
    Ghosts / by Michael Martin.
    p. cm.—(Edge books. The unexplained)
    Includes bibliographical references and index.
    Contents: The mysterious world of ghosts—History of ghosts—Searching for ghosts—Looking for answers.
    ISBN-13: 978-0-7368-2717-1 (hardcover)
    ISBN-10: 0-7368-2717-X (hardcover)
    1. Ghosts—Juvenile literature. [1. Ghosts.] I. Title. II. Series.
BF1461.M365 2005
133.1—dc22   2003024296

Editorial Credits
Carrie A. Braulick, editor; Juliette Peters, designer; Kelly Garvin, photo researcher;
    Eric Kudalis, product planning editor

Photo Credits
Corbis/Bettmann, 10, 23; Lester Lefkowitz, 15
Fortean Picture Library, cover, 17, 18; Janet and Colin Bord, 27; Philip Carr, 14; Tony
    O'Rahilly, 29
Grant L. Robertson Inc., 6
Houserstock/Dave G. Houser, 5
Mary Evans Picture Library, 9, 13; Andrew Green, 26; Harry Price, 19; Julie and Mark
    Hunt, 22
The Myrtles Plantation, 6 (inset)
Scott Flagg, 21, 25

1 2 3 4 5 6 09 08 07 06 05 04

Table of Contents

Chapter 1

The Mysterious World of Ghosts

Old oak trees lead to the house on Oak Alley Plantation in Vacherie, Louisiana. Visitors come to the plantation to learn about how Southerners lived in the early 1800s. But Oak Alley is known for more than its rich history. It is famous for ghost sightings.

Many people have reported ghosts at Oak Alley. Some visitors say they have seen the ghost of a woman walking outside the house. One person claimed to see three ghosts fighting. One of the ghosts was thrown off the second-floor balcony.

Learn about:
• Oak Alley Plantation
• Myrtles Plantation
• Ghost stories

Oak trees line the path leading to the
house at Oak Alley Plantation.

Myrtles
Plantation

Some people believe this photo shows the ghost of Chloe (near right pillar) at Myrtles Plantation. ►

People also have reported strange happenings at the plantation. Workers say the house lights turn on and off during tours. Visitors have heard a child crying when no children were nearby.

Southern Louisiana is also home to Myrtles Plantation. People say the plantation is one of the most haunted places in the United States. Visitors say they have seen ghosts of children playing. Some people have reported seeing the ghost of a slave named Chloe who once lived there. Past owners said they saw a woman's ghost walk up the stairs carrying a candle. Other people have reported hearing the piano play while no one was near it.

About Ghosts

People have told ghost stories for thousands of years. Some stories are about helpful ghosts. Other stories tell of evil ghosts. Some stories are about ghosts that communicate with people.

Millions of people say they have seen ghosts. No one can fully explain all ghost reports. Researchers continue to study reports to learn more about ghosts.

Chapter 2

History of Ghosts

One of the earliest known ghost stories is from Athens, Greece. It is more than 2,000 years old. The story is about a man named Athenodorus. Athenodorus rented a house others said was haunted. One day, he heard a rattling noise. He then saw the ghost of a sad old man in chains. The ghost led Athenodorus into the garden. The ghost pointed at the ground and disappeared.

Learn about:
- The story of Athenodorus
- Margaret and Kate Fox
- Spiritualism

Athenodorus saw the ghost
of an old man in chains.

Lincoln's Ghost

Abraham Lincoln became the U.S. president in 1861. He was shot while attending a theater performance in 1865. He later died.

Since Lincoln's death, many people have claimed that they saw his ghost in the White House. Grace Coolidge was the first person to report Lincoln's ghost. Grace was the wife of President Calvin Coolidge. She claimed to see Lincoln's ghost staring out a window. A White House worker claimed to see Lincoln's ghost pull on his boots while sitting on his bed. Past U.S. Presidents Franklin Roosevelt and Dwight Eisenhower also reported seeing or sensing Lincoln's ghost. Lincoln's ghost was reported most often between 1932 and 1945.

Lincoln's bedroom at the White House

The next day, workers dug up the garden. They found a skeleton in rusty chains. They buried the bones at a graveyard. Athenodorus did not see the ghost again after the bones were properly buried.

A Strange Appearance

Some stories tell of ghosts appearing to loved ones. A famous example occurred in 1250. Englishman William Longsword was fighting in a series of wars called the Crusades. These wars took place in the Middle East between the late 1000s and 1500s. Longsword's mother lived in England. One day, she saw an image of her son. She told her friends about the appearance.

Six months later, a messenger visited Longsword's mother. The messenger told her that her son had died in Egypt. Longsword had died the same day the ghost appeared.

Poltergeists

Some ghosts are poltergeists. These ghosts make noises. They usually are more active than other ghosts. People have reported poltergeists that move objects through the air. Poltergeists have also been known to start fires.

In 1848, sisters Margaret and Kate Fox reported poltergeist activity in Hydesville, New York. They heard loud rapping noises at their home. The raps seemed to answer back when they clapped their hands.

The girls' family set up a code to communicate with the poltergeist. Different numbers of knocks meant different letters of the alphabet. The Fox family said the poltergeist told them it was the spirit of a murdered man.

Later, Margaret and Kate held shows that convinced some people that they could communicate with ghosts. The two sisters performed their acts throughout the United States.

▲ Kate (left) and Margaret (right) Fox performed shows throughout the United States. Their sister, Leah (middle), worked as their manager.

Spiritualism

The idea that people could communicate with ghosts led to a religion called Spiritualism. People around the world tried to communicate with the dead. People who seemed best at communicating with ghosts were called mediums.

Spiritualism was popular until the early 1900s. People lost interest in the religion because many mediums proved to be fake.

Spiritualism led to other types of ghost research. Some people claimed to be ghost photographers. They set up their cameras so ghostlike images would appear in the pictures.

▼ In the early 1900s, many people set up fake ghost photographs.

In the 1970s, channeling became popular. People who performed this activity said they allowed ghosts to take control of their bodies.

Gettysburg National Cemetery

Many people have reported ghosts at Gettysburg National Cemetery in Pennsylvania. More soldiers died in the Battle of Gettysburg than in any other battle of the Civil War (1861–1865).

Reports include ghost soldiers acting out battles, unusual scents, and poltergeist activity. Many other reports are about ghosts of sick soldiers. The ghosts are reported in a building once used as a hospital. Pictures taken at Gettysburg sometimes have unusual figures or light spots.

Today, people can take ghost tours near the cemetery. Tour guides tell the visitors about famous sightings.

Chapter 3
Searching for Ghosts

People who investigate hauntings are called ghost hunters. Some ghost hunters form clubs. These groups include the American Ghost Society and the Ghost Research Society.

A British man named Harry Price was a well-known ghost hunter in the early 1920s. Price's most famous case involved the Borley Rectory. Priests, nuns, and other church leaders lived at this house. It was known as the most haunted house in England. People reported an image of a carriage pulled by two ghostly horses near the house. People also said they heard unusual noises and saw ghosts in the house.

Learn about:
- Famous ghost hunters
- Borley Rectory
- Ghost hunting equipment

The Borley Rectory is one of England's most famous haunted buildings.

Price began investigating Borley Rectory in 1929. During his investigation, Price experienced strange happenings. He heard knocks and ringing bells. He saw objects fly through the air.

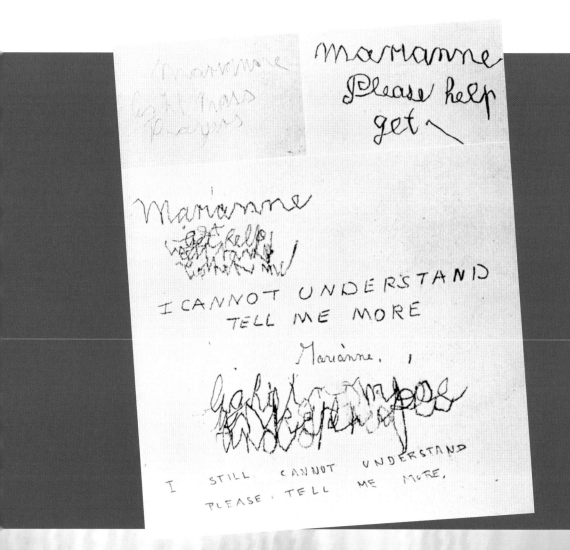

↑ Some people say Borley Rectory's ghost scribbled on the walls.

After years of study, Price said a murdered nun probably caused most of the ghostly events. She had died about 600 years before Price studied the rectory.

Hans Holzer

Hans Holzer is one of today's famous ghost hunters. Holzer often uses psychics in his investigations. Psychics claim to see and hear things that others do not.

Holzer brings psychics to a place he is studying. He does not tell them anything about the place. The psychics sometimes supply important information for Holzer's studies. Holzer has written several books about psychics and hauntings.

▼ Harry Price was a well-known ghost hunter.

Equipment

Ghost hunters carry equipment to help them study ghosts. They sometimes carry thermometers. People who claim to see ghosts often report a chill in the air. In 1998, the temperature in an area being studied dropped more than 50 degrees Fahrenheit (28 degrees Celsius).

Ghost researchers also use tape recorders. Researchers sometimes hear mysterious voices when they play the tapes.

Some researchers believe ghosts' energy gives off unusual magnetic fields. People can use equipment to detect magnetic forces in these areas. Ghost hunters sometimes use magnetic field detectors during their studies.

▲ Ghost hunters use a variety of equipment
to search for signs of ghosts.

Cameras

Many ghost hunters carry cameras. They take pictures during their investigations. Some researchers have developed photos that show ghostlike images. Many of these researchers say they noticed nothing unusual while taking the pictures.

Video camera recordings sometimes show glowing balls of light. The balls of light glide through the air.

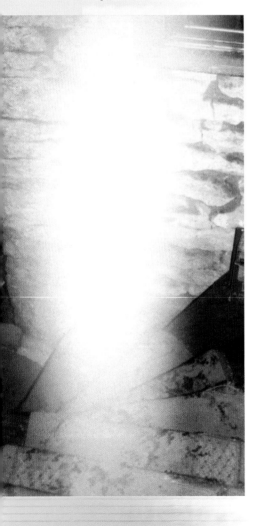

▼ **Ghostlike images that look like sprays of mist appear in some pictures.**

The Borden Murders

In 1892, Andrew and Abby Borden were killed in their home with an ax in Fall River, Massachusetts. Police arrested Andrew's daughter Lizzie for the murders. She was found not guilty in court. Since the murders, people have told stories that the house is haunted. Today, the home is a museum.

Ghost researcher Katherine Ramsland and a museum tour guide recently went to the basement of the Borden home. Ramsland turned on her tape recorder. She asked if anyone else was there with them. Ramsland and the guide heard nothing. But when they played the tape, they heard a gruff voice answer them.

Borden home

Chapter 4

Looking for Answers

Scientists try to find reasons for believing or not believing that a reported haunting is true. They look for a way to explain what happened.

Theories

Some scientists believe that certain people can move objects with their minds. This ability is called psychokinesis, or PK. The scientists think PK can explain poltergeist and other ghostlike activity.

Learn about:
- Psychokinesis
- Magnetic fields
- Fake ghost photos

Ghost researchers investigate
reported hauntings to explain them.

EDGE FACT

⬆ The photographer of this photo said he did not see the ghostlike person when he took the photo.

Some ghost hunters believe ghosts can communicate by using magnetic fields. This theory would explain how sound on a tape recorder can be recorded when no sound was heard. They think ghosts can record the sounds without speaking.

Scientists think some people imagine seeing ghosts. People who are mentally ill or tired can see things that aren't really there. People also may imagine ghost sightings after taking drugs.

Ghostlike images have appeared on thousands of photos. Reflections and shadows can cause these images. Some people make photos with ghostlike images to attract attention.

⬇ **Some people create fake ghost photos with white sheets.**

Explaining Ghost Sightings

Most ghost reports can be explained. A noise may be caused by bats in an attic or by branches scraping against a window. A person may play a joke to make others believe a ghost is present.

Most ghost researchers believe less than 10 percent of ghost reports are completely unexplained. But researchers try to study as many reports as possible. Each new case can help them understand more about ghosts.

▲ Ghost photos and other evidence can help
researchers find out if a report is true.

Glossary

magnetic field (mag-NE-tik FEELD)—the space near a magnetic body or current-carrying body in which magnetic forces can be detected

medium (MEE-dee-um)—a person who claims to make contact with ghosts

plantation (plan-TAY-shuhn)—a large farm found in warm areas where crops such as coffee, tea, rubber, and cotton are grown

poltergeist (POLE-tuhr-gyst)—a noisy ghost

psychic (SYE-kik)—a person who claims to sense, see, or hear things that others do not; some psychics say they can sense and communicate with ghosts.

psychokinesis (SYE-ko-kuh-nee-sis)—the ability to move objects with the mind

rectory (REK-tuh-ree)—a building where church leaders live

Spiritualism (SPIHR-uh-choo-uh-li-zuhm)—a religion based on the belief that people can talk to spirits of the dead

Read More

Oxlade, Chris. *The Mystery of Haunted Houses.* Can Science Solve? Des Plaines, Ill.: Heinemann, 2000.

Watkins, Graham. *Ghosts and Poltergeists.* Unsolved Mysteries. New York: Rosen, 2002.

Internet Sites

FactHound offers a safe, fun way to find Internet sites related to this book. All of the sites on FactHound have been researched by our staff.

Here's how:

1. Visit *www.facthound.com*
2. Type in this special code **073682717X** for age-appropriate sites. Or enter a search word related to this book for a more general search.
3. Click on the **Fetch It** button.

FactHound will fetch the best sites for you!

Index

WOODLAND HIGH SCHOOL
800 N. MOSELEY DRIVE
STOCKBRIDGE, GA 30281
(770) 389-2784